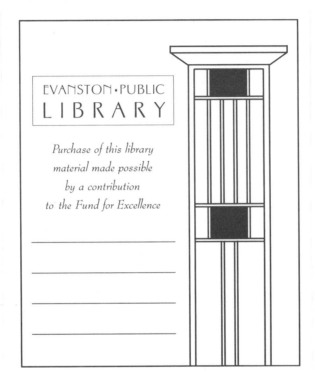

EVANSTON·PUBLIC
LIBRARY

Purchase of this library
material made possible
by a contribution
to the Fund for Excellence

_____

_____

_____

_____

SHRIMP

A Buddy Book by
Deborah Coldiron

ABDO
Publishing Company

UNDERWATER WORLD

VISIT US AT
www.abdopublishing.com

Published by ABDO Publishing Company, 8000 West 78th Street, Edina, Minnesota 55439.

Copyright © 2008 by Abdo Consulting Group, Inc. International copyrights reserved in all countries. No part of this book may be reproduced in any form without written permission from the publisher. Buddy Books™ is a trademark and logo of ABDO Publishing Company.

Printed in the United States.

Coordinating Series Editor: Sarah Tieck
Contributing Editor: Michael P. Goecke
Graphic Design: Deborah Coldiron
Cover Photograph: Medio Images
Interior Photographs/Illustrations: Art Explosion (page 17); Clipart.com (pages 13, 15); Brandon Cole Marine Photography (pages 21, 25); ImageMix (pages 7, 16, 17, 29); Minden Pictures: Fred Bavendam (pages 19, 23, 27, 28), Mitsuaki Iwago page 17), Frans Lanting (page 5), David Wachenfeld/Auscape (page 9), Birgitte Wilms (page 11) Norbert Wu (page 19); Photos.com (pages 17, 253); Professor David Scholnick (page 30); Stockbyte (page 16)

Library of Congress Cataloging-in-Publication Data

Coldiron, Deborah.
    Shrimp / Deborah Coldiron.
        p. cm. — (Underwater World)
    Includes index.
    ISBN 978-1-59928-814-7
    1. Shrimps—Juvenile literature. I. Title.

QL444.M33C63 2007
595.3'88—dc22

                                                                2007014854

Table Of Contents

The World Of Shrimp

Every living creature needs water. Some animals not only need water, they live in it, too.

Scientists have found more than 250,000 kinds of plants and animals living underwater. And, they believe there could be one million more! The shrimp is one animal that lives in this underwater world.

Seventy percent of Earth's surface is covered in water.

There are at least 2,000 different **species** of shrimp. These small **invertebrates** are found in both salt water and freshwater.

Shrimp come in many colors, patterns, and sizes. The smallest shrimp are less than one inch (three cm) long. The largest can be more than 12 inches (30 cm) long!

Most shrimp are gray, brown, white, or pink. But, some species come in bright colors like red and blue!

Shrimp live in lakes, rivers, and oceans. There are saltwater and freshwater shrimp.

Generally, most shrimp are bottom dwellers. They spend most of their lives on sand or mud deep underwater.

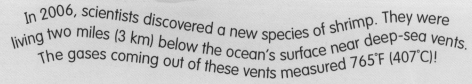

In 2006, scientists discovered a new species of shrimp. They were living two miles (3 km) below the ocean's surface near deep-sea vents. The gases coming out of these vents measured 765°F (407°C)!

A few species of shrimp are unusual because they live in large groups. These groups, or schools, often swim long distances together.

The Creature's Features

Like other **crustaceans** (kruhs-TAY-shuhns), the shrimp's body is covered in a tough shell. This shell is called an exoskeleton. It helps protect the shrimp's soft body.

A shrimp will outgrow this hard shell many times in its life. When this happens, the shrimp molts, or takes off its shell. This makes room for a new shell that has grown underneath.

FAST FACTS Molting is not easy! Sometimes a shrimp loses one or more of its legs while molting. But over time, the leg usually grows back.

Many shrimp eat their old shell after they molt. The shell is a healthy food for shrimp.

A shrimp's body is designed to move. It has ten pairs of legs. Five pairs of legs are designed for walking. The other five help it swim.

Shrimp also have three pairs of short arms. These help them eat.

Even though shrimp have eyes, they don't see very well. This is why they have four antennae, or feelers, on their heads. These antennae help shrimp taste and touch.

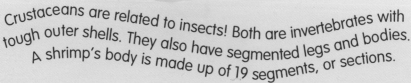

FAST FACTS Crustaceans are related to insects! Both are invertebrates with tough outer shells. They also have segmented legs and bodies. A shrimp's body is made up of 19 segments, or sections.

The Body Of A Shrimp

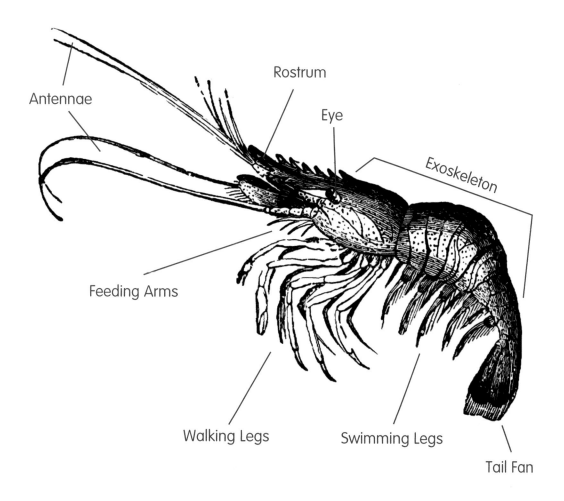

Antennae

Rostrum

Eye

Exoskeleton

Feeding Arms

Walking Legs

Swimming Legs

Tail Fan

A Shrimp's Life

Shrimp begin their lives as tiny eggs. A female shrimp can lay thousands of eggs at one time. Until the eggs are ready to hatch, most shrimp mothers carry them with their swimming legs.

When the baby shrimp hatch, they float to the surface. Larger fish and whales eat 80 percent of them. Still, many survive and become adults.

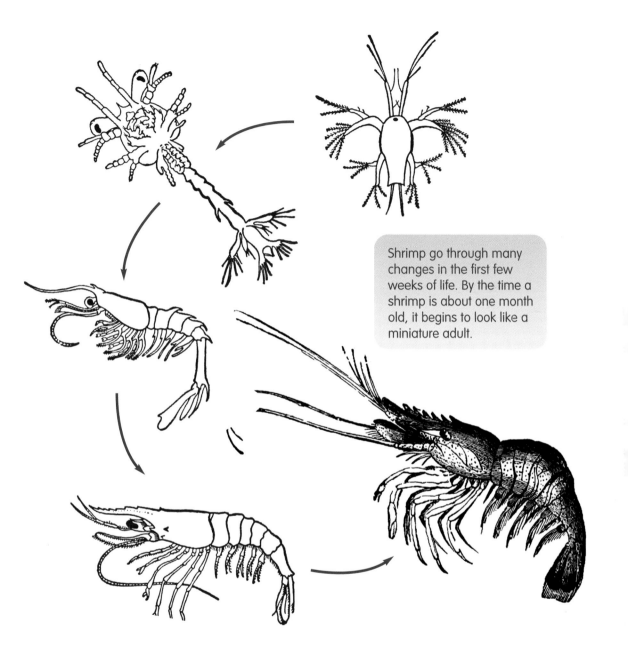

Shrimp go through many changes in the first few weeks of life. By the time a shrimp is about one month old, it begins to look like a miniature adult.

Family Business

Shrimp belong to a group of animals called **crustaceans**. There are around 42,000 known **species** of crustaceans! For example, crabs and lobsters are crustaceans.

All crustaceans have outer shells for protection. Also, crustacean legs and bodies are made up of small parts called segments.

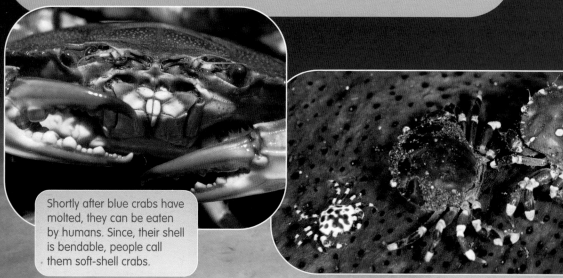

Shortly after blue crabs have molted, they can be eaten by humans. Since, their shell is bendable, people call them soft-shell crabs.

The sally lightfoot crab can be found on the coasts of the Galapogos Islands, near Ecuador.

Lobsters come in a variety of colors. But, nearly all lobsters turn red when cooked. Only albino lobsters keep their original color.

Lobsters can regrow lost legs, claws, and antennae. In fact, lobsters sometimes drop a claw to confuse a predator while they escape.

Hermit crabs adopt abandoned seashells to use as houses. These crabs have soft bodies. So, a seashell provides a strong shelter for protection.

Commensal crabs are often found living inside the bodies of sea cucumbers! These small crustaceans cause the cucumber no harm.

Krill are shrimplike crustaceans. They are an important food source for many animals, including baleen whales and whale sharks.

Dinnertime

Different types of shrimp eat different things. Most shrimp eat both plants and animals. Some small shrimp eat only plants, such as algae.

Many shrimp are **scavengers**. They eat bits of dead plants and animals that have drifted down from above.

Algae often covers large areas of the ocean floor. Animals such as starfish feed on algae.

Many animals, including crabs, scavenge the seafloor for food.

Some shrimp eat tiny floating sea creatures called plankton. Other shrimp, such as cleaner shrimp, eat **parasites** from the bodies of living fish.

Shrimp are also powerful predators. Harlequin shrimp eat only starfish. Usually, small harlequin shrimp work in pairs to turn over the large starfish!

Harlequin shrimp have unusual paddle-shaped arms and wildly spotted skin. They are talented starfish hunters.

Friends And Neighbors

Shrimp have many strange and interesting neighbors. Often their neighbors help protect them.

Pistol shrimp make great underwater roommates. They dig tunnels into the sand and share their homes with goby fish. Gobies offer protection by guarding the tunnel's opening. They serve as "eyes" for pistol shrimp, which are blind.

Goby fish keep watch while pistol shrimp work on their tunnels.

Anemone shrimp make their homes among the stinging **tentacles** of **sea anemones**. Anemone shrimp are immune to the sea anemone's **toxins**. And, the sea anemone's tentacles protect them from predators.

Some fish are also able to hide safely among stinging sea anemones.

Enemies And Threats

Shrimp are food for many of Earth's underwater creatures. Birds, animals, and even people also eat shrimp.

Seals hunt shrimp that live in cold waters. Small sharks, such as the whitetip reef shark, prey on shrimp living near reefs.

Whitetip Reef Shark

Humans hunt for shrimp using large nets called trawls. But these nets often trap many other animals, such as sea turtles and squid. Also, they can damage a shrimp's home.

A shrimp can use its powerful tail to jet backward. This helps it quickly escape predators!

Fascinating Facts

👉 In 2005, scientists were surprised to find the Jurassic shrimp living in the Coral Sea. They thought it had vanished 50 million years ago!

A pistol shrimp

👉 A pistol shrimp can use its claw to make a loud noise. The noise can kill small fish or break glass up to five feet (2 m) away!

🦐 Ground-up shrimp shells are being used to create bandages! The U.S. Army already uses them!

🦐 Some shrimp can change their body color to help them hide from predators. This is called camouflage.

Crinoid shrimp use camouflage to hide in their surroundings.

Learn And Explore

Some people study shrimp for a living. Professor David Scholnick is a biologist from Pacific University in Oregon. He invented a shrimp **treadmill**.

Scholnick found that healthy shrimp can run or swim for hours without getting tired! Shrimp that are sick move much slower. This makes it easier for predators to catch them.

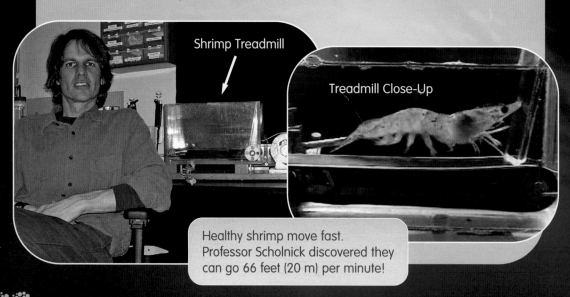

Shrimp Treadmill

Treadmill Close-Up

Healthy shrimp move fast. Professor Scholnick discovered they can go 66 feet (20 m) per minute!

IMPORTANT WORDS

crustacean any of a group of animals with hard shells that live mostly in water. Crabs, lobsters, and shrimp are all crustaceans.

invertebrate an animal without a backbone.

parasite an animal or a plant that lives in or on a host.

scavenger an animal that eats dead animals that it did not kill.

species living things that are very much alike.

tentacle a long, slender body part that grows around the mouth or the head of some animals.

toxin a poison.

treadmill a machine with a moving belt used for exercise.

WEB SITES

To learn more about shrimp, visit ABDO Publishing Company on the World Wide Web. Web sites about shrimp are featured on our Book Links page. These links are routinely monitored and updated to provide the most current information available.

www.abdopublishing.com

INDEX